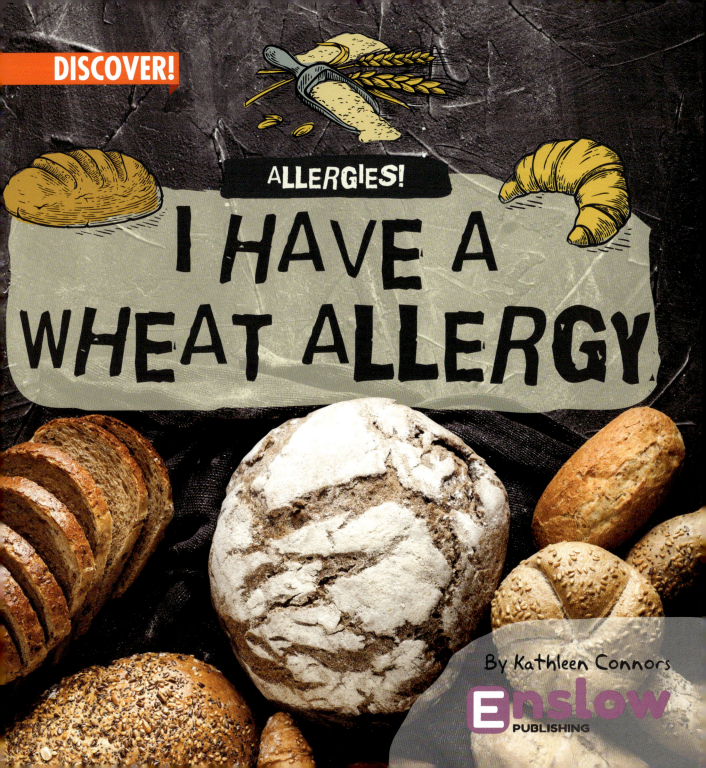

DISCOVER!

ALLERGIES!

I HAVE A WHEAT ALLERGY

By Kathleen Connors

Enslow
PUBLISHING

Please visit our website, www.enslow.com. For a free color catalog of all our high-quality books, call toll free 1-800-398-2504 or fax 1-877-980-4454.

Library of Congress Cataloging-in-Publication Data

Names: Connors, Kathleen, author.
Title: I have a wheat allergy / Kathleen Connors.
Description: Buffalo, New York : Enslow Publishing, [2024] | Series:
   Allergies! | Includes bibliographical references and index. | Audience:
   Grades K-1
Identifiers: LCCN 2022045129 (print) | LCCN 2022045130 (ebook) | ISBN
   9781978533875 (library binding) | ISBN 9781978533868 (paperback) | ISBN
   9781978533882 (ebook)
Subjects: LCSH: Food allergy in children–Juvenile literature. |
   Wheat–Health aspects–Juvenile literature.
Classification: LCC RJ386.5 .C6637 2024 (print) | LCC RJ386.5 (ebook) |
   DDC 618.92/975–dc23/eng/20220928
LC record available at https://lccn.loc.gov/2022045129
LC ebook record available at https://lccn.loc.gov/2022045130

Portions of this work were originally authored by Maria Nelson and published as *I'm Allergic to Wheat*. All new material this edition authored by Kathleen Connors.

Published in 2024 by
Enslow Publishing
2544 Clinton Street
Buffalo, NY 14224

Designer: Claire Wrazin
Editor: Kristen Nelson

Photo credits: Cover (photo) Nikolay Litov/Shutterstock.com; Cover (art), pp. 3, 4, 12, 14, 18, 22 Vectorgoods studio/Shutterstock.com; Series Art (texture) arigato/Shutterstock.com; p. 5 Galigrafiya/Shutterstock.com; Art (wheat) pp. 6, 20 bioraven/Shutterstock.com; p. 7 Pearl PhotoPix/Shutterstock.com; p. 9 Alexander_Safonov/Shutterstock.com; p. 11 onstockphoto/Shutterstock.com; p. 13 fizkes/Shutterstock; p. 15 George Rudy/Shutterstock; p. 17 Charles Knowles/Shutterstock; p. 19 Diana Taliun/Shutterstock.com; p. 21 Stephen Barnes/Shutterstock.com

Printed in the United States of America

Some of the images in this book illustrate individuals who are models. The depictions do not imply actual situations or events.

CPSIA compliance information: Batch #CS24ENS: For further information contact Enslow Publishing, at 1-800-398-2504.

Find us on

CONTENTS

Boldface words appear in Words to Know.

COMMON ALLERGY

Does eating toast make you itch? Do your eyes get watery after you have a cookie? It could be a wheat allergy. Wheat is one of the most common food allergies in children. Many children outgrow it too!

If someone in your family has an allergy, you're more likely to have one.

5

WHAT'S A REACTION?

An allergic **reaction** happens when the body **identifies** something that's commonly harmless as harmful. It creates special parts of the blood called antibodies to fight it. In wheat allergies, the body is fighting a **protein** found in wheat.

Wheat we eat comes in many forms, including wheat bran and flour.

An allergic reaction to wheat may start a few minutes to a few hours after someone has eaten a food with wheat in it. Reactions include an itchy feeling in the mouth or throat. Some people might have a stuffy nose and watery eyes.

Wheat allergies are found more often in children than adults.

9

Hives may also be part of an allergic reaction to wheat. The worst allergic reaction is called anaphylaxis (aa-nuh-fuh-LAK-suhs). It may include a tight feeling in the chest and throat, trouble breathing, and passing out.

Hives are raised, itchy patches of skin that are redder or paler than the skin around them.

AVOID WHEAT

A drug called epinephrine (eh-puh-NEH-fruhn) is used to treat anaphylaxis and other bad reactions. But, the best way to control a wheat allergy is to avoid, or stay away from, foods with wheat in them.

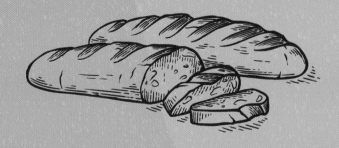

It can be hard to have a food allergy. Always let those around you know so you can stay safe.

Cookies, cake, and bread are most often made with flour from wheat. Pasta, breakfast cereals, and crackers are too. If you have a wheat allergy, it's best if you don't eat these foods.

Many bakeries and stores now carry baked goods not made with wheat—just ask about it!

15

CHECK THE LABEL

If you aren't sure what's in a food, check the label before eating it. The label will say it has wheat in it. It may also say the food was produced near wheat. These foods can cause allergic reactions too!

16

	Calories	2,000	2,500
Total Fat	Less than	65g	80g
Sat. Fat	Less than	20g	25g
Cholesterol	Less than	300mg	300mg
Sodium	Less than	2,400mg	2,400mg
Potassium		3,500mg	3,500mg
Total Carbohydrate		300g	375g
Dietary Fiber		25g	30g

Ingredients: Sugar, corn flour blend (whole grain yellow corn flour, degerminated yellow corn flour, wheat flour, whole grain oat flour, oat fiber, soluble corn fiber, contains 2% or less of partially hydrogenated vegetable oil (coconut, soybean and/or cottonseed), salt, red 40, natural flavor, blue 2, turmeric color, yellow 6, annatto color, blue 1, BHT for freshness.

Vitamins and Minerals: Vitamin C (sodium ascorbate and ascorbic acid), niacinamide, reduced iron, zinc oxide, vitamin B_6 (pyridoxine hydrochloride), vitamin B_2 (riboflavin), vitamin B (thiamin

---

ilk contributes
tassium,
4g Protein.
00 calorie diet.
depending on

	2,500
	80g
	25g
	300mg
	2,400mg
	3,500mg
	375g
	30g

35%

sugar, rice flour,
wheat flour, high
ey, artificial flavor,
l oil with TBHQ for
oda, niacinamide*,
soy lecithin, vitamin
HT (a preservative),

Ketchup, ice cream, and potato chips could contain wheat! Always read the label.

DIFFERENT GRAINS

People allergic to wheat may be allergic to other grains too. Barley, oats, and rye contain similar proteins to those in wheat. These grains are a great **substitute** for wheat if your body doesn't react to them.

Almond flour is sometimes used in place of wheat flour in bread and baked goods.

19

DON'T GET CONFUSED

Wheat allergies and celiac **disease** may seem similar. But, celiac disease isn't a food allergy and causes different problems than wheat allergies. Those with celiac disease get sick because of a protein in wheat called gluten.

20

100% WHEAT & GLUTEN FREE

Products labeled gluten-free may be safe for people with wheat allergies, but not always. Check the label!

WORDS TO KNOW

disease: An illness.

identify: To recognize.

protein: One of the building blocks of food.

reaction: Something that happens when the body is affected by a food, usually in a bad way.

substitute: Something that takes the place of something else.

FOR MORE INFORMATION

BOOKS

Orlando, Amanda. *The Easy Allergy-free Cookbook: 85 Recipes Without Gluten, Dairy, Tree Nuts, Peanuts, Eggs, Fish, Shellfish, Soy, Or Wheat.* Emeryville, CA: Rockridge Press, 2022.

Vallepur, Shalini. *I'm Allergic to Wheat.* King's Lynn, UK: BookLife Publishing, 2019.

WEBSITES

Gluten-Free Kids Recipes

www.celiaccentral.org/kids/recipes/
Find recipes that are safe for those with wheat allergies because they don't use wheat products or products that have been processed with wheat.

Wheat Allergy

kidshealth.org/parent/medical/allergies/wheat_allergy.html
Check out this website to learn more about having a wheat allergy and living with it.

INDEX